I'D RATHER BE HAPPY AND PEE

Release What No Longer Serves You

Maya Lynne Robinson

I'd Rather Be Happy And Pee
(Release What No Longer Serves You)
2nd EDITION
Copyright © 2022 by Maya Lynne Robinson
Cover Art: PhoebeLimArt
Author Photo: Allen Zaki

All rights reserved. Printed in the United States of America. No part of this book may be used or reproduced in any manner whatsoever without written permission except in the case of brief quotations included in articles or reviews.

For information contact us at:
liveintruthinfo@gmail.com

ISBN: 978-1-7374700-2-1
First Edition : December 2021

This book is for the Meek.

May you inherit the Earth.

WHY THIS BOOK?

So why should you read/share/buy this book? I am a daughter, a friend, a partner, a business owner, and an artist. I can see things from the head and the heart to the soul. I don't judge, nor do I claim to have all the answers.

I have battled anxiety and depression. Often crippled by a lack of confidence and trust inside of me, it used to leave me in knots, unable to make a decision and scared to ask for advice. As a black woman, I am expected to be strong at all times and able to withstand anything.

People know me for the strong characters on stage and TV; I am those women. They live in me. However, I am also relatively introverted. Having to wear the mask that everything was okay in my life wears me down to the point I craved only solitude while searching for peace. And then one day, as I was in the bathroom, I realized that my entire body was tense, and one word popped into my head- release. I begin to cry. I didn't want to hold anymore- my pain, fear, or anything that no longer served me.

Sitting on the floor, I began to cry tears of relief. I realized what was holding me back. It was me.

This book is my way of speaking from the heart, letting you guys into my personal life. As I write from the heart, I hope this book inspires you and helps you in your growth process. Go into healing mode. With the support of a spiritual healer and a therapist, I began to heal my wounds instead of burying them.

How can I help? I have something to say that transcends me. The messages come not only for you but for me too.

We all require active listening, problem-solving skills, accountability, and authenticity. People know when you are bullshitting them, and I am not a bullshitter. That's why I want to help.

I wanted to put out a great book to help those who want a bit more of a private inspirational experience like I did. I wanted the reader to have the ability to turn to any page and words become relevant and helpful to their lives. So I'd Rather Be Happy and Pee was written because affirmations and inspirations are motivational help. Daily saying and reading affirmations have made all the difference in managing anxiety and stress.

I hope this book helps you put a positive spin on crappy situations and focus on what you want, not your lack. Faith over fear wins.

These are some of my most precious thoughts and feelings on life and how I turned my problems into prospers. It's never too late to start thinking in affirming ways.

Enjoy the climb and the dips. Enjoy the ride. This book has been a labor of love to release what no longer was serving me.

WHY ME?

Sharing anything personal is scary. I once was taught when people see you have an issue in your life, they have found your weakness. I wasn't afraid to write about any obstacles I overcame; I was worried about people thinking I would preach or judge them. Openly, I cried, laughed, and did a lot of cussing as I wrote and rewrote. I was uncomfortable with how much I was willing to write and share about my life.

2015 was the most brutal year of my life. I went from the most dramatic high to the most cringe-worthy low. I didn't understand why life was happening the way it was for me – I lost everything.

By September, I began to journal. Working multiple jobs and acting in plays while auditioning was not paying the rent. I was creating Motivational Monday posts and getting excellent feedback. I try to live my life from a place of gratitude, giving back however I can. I saw social media "likes" and positive comments, and it felt good. I felt my words were helping others, as well as myself.

The task of weekly positivity was difficult at times. It began to feel like work to find quotes; it was no longer the fun and the organic project I had intended. Pretty much, I didn't feel like doing it at times. And so, I stopped.

What I hadn't realized was I'd created a world where I now had a responsibility to design, build, and share positivity. In my absence, people felt like I abandoned them or, worse, myself.

It's about affirming your intentions as opposed to the handling of obstacles. It's about speaking from the heart and inspiring others to feel safe to do so, as well. It's about healing generational trauma and finding the light and the love within. Sometimes a quote or a thought can spark something in you at just the right time.

Enjoy this book. Write in it. Highlight it. Read it page by page or open it at random. Use it as an aid to receive owning your power and soul's mission.

I wish you a positive, motivational and authentic journey.

CHAPTERS

WHY THIS BOOK? III

WHY ME? VI

CHAPTERS IX

I AM 13

I AM APPRECIATIVE 15

I AM AWARE 17

I AM BEAUTIFUL 19

I AM BOSSY 21

I AM BRAVE 23

I AM CHARITABLE 26

I AM CLEAR 28

I AM CONFIDENT 31

I AM DIVINE 34

I AM DRIVEN 36

I AM EMOTIONAL 38

CHECK IN #1	40
I AM ENOUGH	42
I AM ETHICAL	44
I AM FORGIVING	47
I AM FREE	49
I AM FUNNY	51
I AM GENEROUS	53
I AM GRATEFUL	55
I AM GROWING	57
I AM HAPPY	61
I AM HEALTHY	64
I AM HONEST	67
I AM HUMBLE	69
I AM KIND	72
CHECK IN #2	74
I AM LEARNING	76
I AM LOGICAL	79
I AM LOVING	82

I AM LOYAL 85

I AM MATURE 88

I AM OPEN 90

I AM PEACE 92

I AM POWERFUL 94

I AM PRACTICAL 96

I AM PRESENT 98

I AM PROGRESS 101

I AM RELAXED 103

CHECK IN #3 105

I AM RESPECTFUL 107

I AM RESPONSIBLE 109

I AM SENSUAL 110

I AM SINCERE 112

I AM SPIRITUAL 113

I AM SUCCESS 115

I AM THRIVING 117

I AM TRIUMPHANT 119

I AM VALUABLE 120

I AM VERSATILE 122

I AM VULNERABLE 124

I AM WISE 127

I AM WORTHY 129

I AM ZEALOUS 133

CHECK IN #4 135

CONCLUSION 138

MANTRA 139

I AM

I have no time, space, or energy to be anyone other than me…

off-camera.

How people react to you isn't your problem. To thine own self be true. Nobody ever says they were happy to have lived their lives the way others wanted them to live. We are all born with our own unique mission; to be the best version of ourselves.

Who the heck told you that you weren't good enough as you are and why the heck did you believe them? It used to be easy to listen to others tell me who I was, another perspective outside of myself where I could get constructive analysis.

When you're a performer, you have to get used to performance reviews. It's a part of the job. I learned not to take it personally if negative things were said because there is always something I can do to improve as an artist. But, it still stings when my personality is up for review.

Learning the importance of self-love was hard. Affirming what I wanted and desired and deserved felt selfish. I had to put compassion, kind words, and value into myself. Those weren't taught to me as a child. I didn't realize that I was missing those things as an adult, as well. That's how you get to the I AM. I had to repeatedly learn the lesson until I defined and designed my boundaries. It's the only way to live authentically and healthily.

People will make you into the image that they need/want to fulfill their "I." You become who they need you to be. Do not believe that is your only choice. Do not allow others to tell you who you are. Figure you out.

Who are you? Defining yourself requires a deep look into your strengths, weaknesses, goals, and village. Once you figure those, you show up in life.

When you don't know who you are, nothing else matters. Your purpose doesn't exist. But you are here for a reason. So, sit with yourself and figure out who you are. Self-evaluation is not a team sport.

I AM APPRECIATIVE

Without gratitude, there is no latitude.

Appreciate Everything.

I spent a lot of time obsessing over how I wanted things and people to behave or receive me so that I was comfortable and happy. I used to be very selfish and unforgiving.

Suppose there isn't an appreciation for what you have and the lessons you've learned. In that case, moments won't be precious and irreplaceable. I have failed to acknowledge the blessings I had received, what I already possessed. Nothing was ever enough.

So how do I change this? I started focusing on whether it was good vibes, good advice, or if I could be a good shoulder to cry on. So I focused on supporting others, and being a blessing to other people helped me appreciate what I had. So that changed my perspective and my abundance.

When's the last time you volunteered? When did you last donate to a good cause? When was the last time you offered mentorship or guidance without expecting, wanting, or asking for anything in return?

Serving others is what humanity is supposed to be about; it's human purpose. It is why we are all connected. Hugs, saying thank you, and cards are just small symbols that what we are doing affects and impacts others in profound and beautiful ways.

Appreciation requires us to not focus on ourselves or the results of how our deeds are received but on how our efforts positively impact others. So, if you don't get a thank you, remember that's not why you did it in the first place. Clout should not be the foundation of positive deeds.

Focusing on the positive things and people in our lives helps us manifest great abundance. Appreciation raises our vibration! By acknowledging the needs and feelings of others, we allow each other to feel seen, nurtured, and safe. What a beautiful gift appreciation is! So saying thank you and please can go a long way in making others feel appreciated.

I AM AWARE

Make choices to learn from behaviors, don't just see them.

2020 was a big year. It was one of the most violent, politically charged, and socio-economically painful years I have ever experienced.

Social media became the barometer of awareness to create a human connection. Public allies became private foes. People spoke about racial injustice as police and civilian brutality raged on. People were losing their jobs yet buying homes with the money they weren't paying landlords for months. Many were working the system, and we saw it all.

New rules. I became so aware, so full of discernment about what I could and could not talk about to certain people. I had to trust my intuition that not everybody spoke about the pandemic and racism.

I was so aware of other people's discomfort that I just ignored my discomfort. I wasn't safe to share my germaphobia nor my health and well-being as a Black woman.

We get so caught up in our viewpoints in life that we forget we are also seen through other people's eyes. How you see me reflects you. My reaction to you was your awareness of me. We mirror energy and behavior all the time to bond.

Conversations divided loved ones as private views became public, but isn't that the point? Who said we all had to agree with one another? It's important to know what kind of belief and value systems you are around. You can evolve past people, but you won't recognize it unless the hard conversations are spoken. Awareness is a requirement for these challenging conversations.

I AM BEAUTIFUL

Feel beautiful from the inside out. Glow and Grow.rammarly

Many of us have had a hard time saying or showcasing our beauty. This trepidation isn't because we believe we are not attractive; it is for fear of how others will perceive that visual representation. So what?! Own your greatness!

We fear judgment, harassment, and our innate power, so we choose not to draw attention to ourselves. 'Doing that dim your light thing,' right? Beauty is in the eye of the beholder, and you're just not going to be for everybody. It's okay.

We showcase brains over beauty, sanity over vanity. We slowly dim our glow, our sparkle, our beautiful essence. It affects self-esteem.

Stand a little taller, smile a little wider, feel a little lighter, and others notice. We are visual creatures. We are mirrors.

How we see ourselves is how we treat ourselves. How we treat ourselves is how others treat us. Life is nothing if not a magnified reflection of self. All that to say, there is nothing wrong with finding yourself attractive and letting the world know. However, remember that beauty starts from within, so be good to look good.

I AM BOSSY

Asking for what I want is a boss move, not bossy. Know the difference.

Being a boss means clear direction and clear communication of needs. There are specific actions and behaviors that you will not accept. Telling people your expectations and standing firm with them can make people uncomfortable. What are the first words you hear? "You're so bossy!" No, I have boundaries, but I'm okay with that if you see it as bossy. Know what you want and, respectfully, as well as eloquently, ask others to respect it.

Bosses are leaders. Congratulations trailblazer! There are so many followers that unless one person takes the lead, entire projects, households, and businesses would fall apart. You are a decision-maker, facilitator, and coach.

When your direction is for protection, when you're willing to shoulder the responsibilities, communicate your needs, facilitate the strengths of others, execute excellent leadership skills, and celebrate the successes as a team, you understand what being a good boss entails. You can be a team player and a boss. Don't be afraid to be a boss, be frightened of bad boundaries and blind leadership.

I AM BRAVE

Be brave, not stupid.

Sometimes the bad things in life put you on the path to the best things yet to come. Bravery enlightens.

I like to go on long trail walks that include water. I wouldn't say I like to get wet during these hikes. Soggy shoes can be highly uncomfortable. How do I get from one side of the creek to the other? One day, I noticed that I jumped from rock to rock. I leap, the fewest steps possible. Sometimes I don't quite make it onto the rock, slip, and get wet. Now I have a choice. I can continue to jump from rock to rock, knowing that I'm wet, potentially slip and fall in again, or I can find a more cautious way to cross that might take me longer but is safer. I can walk through the water, too, as a last result, knowing that I'm already wet.

I jump towards the next rock and slip into the water. A third time, I jump and fall into the water. Sometimes, I make it, and sometimes I don't. By the time I get to the car, I am dry. A little bruised because those rocks hurt, but brave, nonetheless.

There are enough outside roadblocks in life trying to knock us down; we do not need to create them for ourselves. So get up, get going and take a chance to go after life fearlessly.

We don't always know how life will turn out. If I focused on my failures, I would never get out of bed. I would never try anything a second time. I would never know the thrill of flourishing through the obstacles.

What I learned from the rocks is I don't know the outcome. What I do know is my mind is powerful. And whatever the result, I always know that I tried and finished and that there are always multiple choices to get to the finish line. I will be tested repeatedly on my strength and ability to know and be true to my path, no matter how slippery the road.

Brave doesn't mean without fear; it merely means continuing forward even when fear is present. It means stepping away from what you know into what you don't know. It means being willing to forgo comfort for the unknown.

Choose your path. Be brave. Change course, if needed. Live outside your comfort zone.

I AM CHARITABLE

Only give if you expect nothing in return.

How can I be of service to someone else? What things do I no longer need physically, mentally, emotionally, or hold onto in my spirit that prevents me from giving back? What do I have to offer? I would spend hours trying to think of ways to serve and support others. Through a very close relationship, I learned the true definition of charity. Sometimes all you can or should offer is support. Sometimes, others must help themselves first.

Years ago, my mother became homeless and didn't want my help. Barely hanging on myself, she decided to go to a shelter and receive VA benefits instead of feeling like a burden to her daughter. She knew that to grow, she would have to take this uncomfortable journey on her own. We would talk often, and I wanted her to know I was there, which was what she needed.

I thought of my mother often during that time. When I had no money and struggled for rent, I remember going to the Union Rescue Mission in downtown Los Angeles. Sometimes I brought a friend who was going through hard times and sometimes I went alone. I worked in the kitchen. Every time, I would drive into the parking lot, passing Skid Row at 5:00 am. My heart was so full. Each time, they asked me if I would be back. Each time I went, there were new people to meet. I could only hope that the previous crew had gotten on their feet.

That's it! That's the actual charity; support from the heart. It is giving something without expecting anything in return. Finding and supporting people and causes you feel passionate about. Once a day or once a year, every little bit counts and helps.

It's a reminder that it might have been a struggle every month to make ends meet, but I did have a roof over my head. I learned to appreciate the kindness of strangers and the support of friends and family. Doing something for someone other than yourself can be so fulfilling.

I AM CLEAR

Become still to become clear.

I don't know about you, but questions can become a cacophony of clutter in my mind. I become overwhelmed and then do nothing. Does this sound familiar?

Clarity is a visceral and visual understanding that balances everything and illuminates what was blurred. It requires you to make choices and then visualize those choices into existence. Whatever you can see, you can have.

I know what opens me and what makes me close off. There are times when I am wrong when I go against my better judgment and choose not to execute discernment. I am not afraid to fail, edit or scrap a complete thought or plan and start again. Clarity involves editing at times. I may or may not be talking about this book.

So many of us stay in situations and lifestyles that do not fulfill us. Dare to dream. We take our paycheck, and we make do with what we are given, never asking ourselves what we want and deserve and what that looks like. We become passive and lose our internal fire. A dream without a plan remains a dream. Being clear means there is a plan in place.

This is how toilet time started. I would sit and make notes about things I wanted to do with my phone. They began as short-term goals, and I asked myself, how can these goals help me in the future? I figured out life from short to long term, which is the opposite of most people. Still, it gave me clarity about what I was putting my energy into and the things that excited me. It gave me clarity in terms of my passions.

Lastly, the closer you get to clarity, the more roadblocks life shoves at you to try and throw you off balance. When you get close to the end, transparency, the journey may seem even more challenging. This is because life wants to make sure you want and are ready for the plan to unfold. You are so close! Breathe and dust yourself off. Stop editing your life before you have whole ideas. Keep dreaming. Keep getting more and more specific. You can have it all when you know what you want.

I AM CONFIDENT

I boldly walk even when the path disappears.

Confidence is authenticity living in your sense of self. It's being aware that there are favorable or not favorable reactions to your existence, acknowledging other people's feelings and thoughts surrounding YOU, all the while choosing to continue on your path because you believe in a greater purpose than their opinion. You are secure within yourself and feel no need to put others down to make yourself feel bigger or better.

When I share something that I know and understand, there is a difference in my speech, posture, and eyes. People notice, gravitate, emulate, and elevate.

Walking your path, unsure of what the destination looks like, can be scary. Activate your solar plexus.

I AM CREATIVE

Creativity is an emotional expression of my thoughts.

As an actor, I create characters. I pick how they talk, move, think, react, and sometimes have creative control over appearances, such as hair and clothing. When everything comes together, the character comes to life.

There is no limit to how to do it or what creativity looks like. Express yourself. It is full of all your intuition, expression, and emotional availability.

We are constantly processing. The logical points can get in the way of what we're feeling. The creative should point to the mind only after the heart and soul have been addressed. Read that again. Creativity stems from passion.

Limits in creativity hold us back. There is no right or wrong when expressing yourself during the creative process; there is only freedom or limits. So let thoughts show you where words should go. I'm not just talking to artists; I'm talking to everyone. Play.

Creativity is our gift to see something in a way that others have yet to imagine or convey. It is subjective and allows us to process and express freely while taking risks. There is first feeling and then thought. Don't limit your feelings by hyper-focusing on your thoughts. Create freely.

I AM DIVINE

Feel other worldly and divine, though you may be human.

Everyone has a purpose, and it is predetermined. Due to free will, we, individually, are the only ones who can mess up our journeys. What we choose to believe and how we behave may have varying effects on how and if we achieve our greatness.

I grew up thinking divinity was religion. I was surrounded by multiple religions: the Baha'i Faith, Christianity, Islam, Judaism, and Buddhism. Through religion, I learned the power of prayer and blessings. What I have found works for me is the celestial sense of spirit guides and the bliss of earthly wonders. I am a spiritual being having a human experience.

There is a connection between us and nature. The ability to give each other life with each breath/release is divinity to me. It is the quality of being reverent. There is a deep and solemn respect for other things and other people's beliefs. Hug a tree, meditate in the park, or water a plant.

Divinity allows me to believe in something good, bigger, and better, guiding me to my best self. We are all connected.

I AM DRIVEN

Hard work hurts, then heals.

I feel most driven when I have so many projects going on, and they all have to be done around the same time. I'm tired and overwhelmed but realize that this is a blessing; it's everything I asked for coming together all at once. And so, I push myself forward.

How often have you been told you could not have something, be something or do something? And then you went out and did it, and became all that and more? Yep, cheers to your drive! Well done!

Many people don't want to cheer you on because they stopped going after what they wanted. So when the road gets hard, you typically feel lonelier because everyone isn't willing to travel the terrain to get to where you are going.

Sometimes you have to plant the seeds, harvest the crop, and cook the meal because you want the taste of success.

We live in a world of instant gratification and desire without being willing to do the long-term work to create a lasting legacy. We have to have ideas and dreams that push us past what we think we want our limits to be. Get a little dirty. Be a little tired. Take a small break. Try until success occurs, but do not, I repeat, do not give up. Rinse and repeat.

I AM EMOTIONAL

Expressed sensitivity is a superpower.

We are not robots, but the world constantly requires us to mask emotions for the sake of success, likes, followers, and friends. For example, in a world of people living life like a photo shoot instead of a photo album, it causes circumstances to distort our genuine emotions for benefit.

We've been taught that you lose power or respect by showcasing emotion. People share less when it comes to emotions because we treat both the person and their feelings as weaknesses. So let's stop normalizing this thought process. We keep trying to protect ourselves from others, knowing what makes us vulnerable and hurts, but it's more important to feel.

When was the last time you shared your pain? It was a social media experiment two years ago, and the results disturbed me. When I posted from a place of positivity, there were fewer likes and less engagement.

When I posted from a place of pain, you guessed it, more people watched, commented, and lurked on my pages. I learned that sharing our shadows broke from the allure of the perfect life.

People enjoy watching people not do or feel well because it makes them feel better about their circumstances. Immediately after that, I decided that I would limit my social media engagement, shelved my documentary about the experiment, and began to limit my reality tv watching.

Why do we fetishize the pain of others? How can we learn to let down our walls, especially after we've opened up and shown vulnerability and then had to close ourselves off again? We are human and require a connection. So, take the time to get real and present where we are and how we feel.

And remember, anyone who causes or relishes in the rollercoaster that is your pain must be removed immediately. Just because you feel and show emotions, it doesn't permit people to manipulate them. Emotions are a gift, not a curse.

CHECK IN #1

So, what am I learning about myself? I'm learning to let go of the little things. I'm learning how to judge well. I'm learning I treasure solitude when healing. It's okay not to want to be with everyone all the time. I am trusting my intuition. I'm learning that I enjoy smaller groups of friends. If it's going to be a big group, I prefer it to be with those I love.

I'm learning that I hate yelling in anger. My body shakes. I'm not too fond of loud noises unless it's bouts of excitement or laughter. I'm learning that I worry a lot. I'm often in my head. I'm learning that I have a pure heart even during great adversity. I am learning to stand my ground when wronged. I am learning to apologize for allowing childhood trauma to dictate my adult life for far too long. When people show me who they are, I am learning to believe them the first time.

I'm learning that not everyone understands that forgiveness does not mean reconciliation. Just because

I let someone go, with or without an apology, it doesn't mean I will allow that someone back in my life.

I am learning to trust with my heart, not just my head, and the importance of listening to learn instead of listening to respond. I am learning to speak to those as I wish to be spoken to. I am learning just how deep and spiritual I am. I no longer want to focus on the past but the present and prepare for the abundant future that has yet to unfold.

But most of all, I am learning that I love who I am as I am. I've changed, in the past, for others, with positive and negative results. I no longer wish to defend who I am nor change to please others.

I AM ENOUGH

Don't pretend to be.

Have you ever gone through life feeling like people will always find fault with you and what you do no matter what you did? Your clothes aren't correct, you talk funny, you're not smart enough? That feeling that other people's expectations of how you should behave and live were supposed to be more critical than your authentic self?

This feeling can leave your heart heavy and your mind in overdrive. But you have the power to control not only how you respond but how you feel about yourself.

Nothing should be more important than your peace of mind. Other people's thoughts should not be more important than yours, and they are also not your problem. I have to live with me for the rest of my life, not you. If I'm not enough, you have other options.

Are you willing to stay true to yourself even if that means losing those you love? I hope so. It can't be more important to lose yourself while keeping people around who don't appreciate what you bring. Stop compromising and changing for people who don't appreciate you for who you truly are.

Failure to listen to that feeling inside or physical response to what is inherently false within you or around you will trip you up and slow you down every time from achieving greatness. Learn yourself and celebrate your enough-ness.

It's much harder to re-find yourself than find the right people, so show up for yourself. If you love who you are, don't change to be someone else's wants. Teach them your truths. If they go because they don't like you as you are, let them go.

I AM ETHICAL

Behave three levels deep- mind, body, and spirit.

I regret going against my gut instincts and morals to appease and to feel included with others. I grew up a people pleaser. If something felt wrong, if I should do or say something, I didn't. I didn't want to be a goody-two-shoes or the moral police. I wanted to be liked. I would get terrible headaches because of not speaking up. I watched the innocent get in trouble because I didn't want to take a stand and insert myself in someone else's situation. I didn't like the backlash of not minding my own business.

Our instincts never lie. They are imperative to our survival. They showcase our morality and force us to face the truth. Rarely something, such as our mental health or physical well-being, isn't sacrificed because of the resistance of illuminating a wrong.

It's important to acknowledge right and wrong so that we don't make the same mistake again. Morality is a subjective process and a collective process. Thoughts and behaviors affect us and those around us and how they think and feel. So be careful about the birds you flock with and be cautious with what you're teaching others to do because people are always watching, thinking, and putting into action what they learn that others get away with

People will do a lot for a little extra, but our moral compass always has a way of coming back and finding us. Be smart, be truthful, and do right by others. So do what is right and not necessarily what is easy.

I have no time for my spirit, body, and mind to all be at war and behave differently. Nor do I allow other people in my inner circle to act as such without open and honest communication about my feelings about their behavior.

What if someone doesn't like being called out? I wait until I am asked, and they often ask. When mind, body, and energy begin to move away from them, people can feel. Inherently, they know why. I don't try to soothe; I try to get to the root, and you should too. Call them out and ask them to do the same for you.

Eventually, everyone slips up when they wear two faces.

I AM FORGIVING

Offer forgiveness even when there is no apology.

The hardest thing for me is to forgive a person who has hurt me. I know it's not my place to judge another person's pain and how they choose to manifest it. My job is to temper my reactions to the hurt.

Forgive yourself and others. We all have faults. Let it take you the time it takes you. Hurt people hurt people, and many people are hurting right now. What is forgiveness? It looks like releasing the power of the words and actions and seeing that someone else's treatment of you is not your fault; it's something within them. We forgive because to hold onto negativity does a disservice to our growth and happiness.

Now, there are times when I have required forgiveness. It's tough, especially when you know you're wrong to say, I apologize, but that's just about ego and pride. When you're wrong, ask forgiveness without blaming others. Hold yourself fully accountable for your actions or words; otherwise, it's a fauxpology.

I want a healthy life and understand that forgiveness does not mean I must welcome people back into my life. Forgiveness and reconciliation can be mistaken for the same, but they are pretty different.

Release the need for inclusion, do it to heal YOU. You cannot, nor are you in charge of, someone else's healing and growth. Holding anger and animosity will make us sick. I wish no one ill will and hope only blessings prosper in their lives.

And, just in case, because we were once in "that place," I choose to do it from afar at times. You will only fool me once. I no longer hold onto the pain and confusion of toxic familiarity.

I AM FREE

I do a thing called What I Want.

Choices. Everybody has them. Nobody owns us. We are more than our physical beings; I'm talking about our souls and spirits, our joy and our pain. We own them. Some people may own our time during the workday, and children may own our time as parents, but we live in a society of choice. So I'm talking about free will because every choice has positive and negative consequences.

People should use our services, but never our souls. If something drains or cages us, we must address it. When what we address is dismissed or disregarded, and when we feel so restricted that our essence dims and fear consumes us, we must learn to fly away. Soar, my friend!

I seriously have had to ask myself; Do I allow others to "own" me? Did I give away too much of myself? Sometimes the silence is deafening as I wait for my reply while already knowing the answer. Yes. Once I knew better, I made better choices. I remember that I deserve to take up space and, in doing so, walk away, re-find myself and grow.

Sometimes walking away doesn't feel free because we're in a state of uncertainty as to what is next. So, when we choose the unknown, we must accept it, own it, and allow it to shape our new reality. Beware of clipping your wings.

Don't give all your power to outside sources. Instead, take accountability for your beliefs, actions, feelings, and how you allowed others to treat you. Take responsibility for allowing another to control how you respond, feel, and think. We all have choices, and we all have voices. Free yourself from the restrictions you gave yourself and for the way you allowed others to make you feel.

I AM FUNNY

Laughter makes conflict easier.

Everyone has a sense of humor, and not everyone will appreciate yours. It's okay! Funny is subjective.

I am the type of person who has difficulty laughing out loud unless I'm taken off guard. An off-color comment or a witty joke will receive a gleam in my eye and a smirk on my face. That's high praise. I'm a challenging sale to make laugh out loud.

It wasn't until 2020 that I began to remember the importance of visual cues for connecting people. With the masks, I no longer could register if I put a smile on someone's face or annoyed them unless they chuckled.

That was my AHA moment. I realized that it's essential to share the joyful noise of laughter with another when communicating. It's how we connect. Laughter is such a beautiful gift that connects and heals.

Laughter fills your body and spirit. Having the ability to tell a joke or story and make another person laugh is not easy. You have to be relatable, have amazing timing, and have the ability to engage your audience. Turn your pain turned into a pun.

Laughter comes when pain meets healing. It is the best medicine.

I AM GENEROUS

Fill your cup, then someone else's. Wash and repeat.

There's a difference between being generous and being taken for granted. The goal of generosity is to give what you can in any way that doesn't leave you without your essential survival needs. So put your mask on first.

I've always wanted to help people so that they don't have to go through or continue to go through the things that I did. I want my loved ones to have a better life. Sometimes that generosity isn't appreciated or respected. When I give, and others willingly take, I deplete if no one fills my cup. Then I have to retreat until I can fill myself up again. Then, one day, I got tired of the pattern. Never again will I give from an empty cup. Never will I allow my spirit to be drained dry and the generosity I provide not be returned. Generosity should not require lack.

My new mantra is: What I want wants me. It is based on mutual generosity in all its forms.

Ask yourself two questions. What am I willing to give? I am eager to give my time to support, a shoulder to cry on, an ear to listen to, and a hand to hold. We can't hold our hands out and expect the world to give us praise for kindness; we must give without requirements.

This leads me to the second question: What are my expectations on how you receive from me? This is where ego can get in the way. You should expect nothing in return, not even a thank you, though that would be appreciated. Giving without the expectation of receiving is one of the highest forms of generosity you can provide to someone else. So suppose you're giving to get something back, including affirmation. In that case, you have to think about if the gift is coming with attachments.

Generosity creates a foundation of unconditional support. Let's be generous in our words and deeds.

I AM GRATEFUL

Always needing more will never leave you full.

Nothing has been handed to me in life. I had to fight for, take and kick down doors to get here. That makes my journey so much more meaningful for me. It also makes me grateful it happened this way because I take no opportunity for granted. I am thankful for this path because it has created the woman I am today.

This is the reason I write. I wanted to be able to one day look back on my journey. This is also the reason I keep a gratitude log. It helps me remember and focus on what I have been blessed with, whether people, places, things, or experiences.

I implore you to rid yourself of the negative self-talk that doesn't serve you. It doesn't serve growth, change, or wisdom. It doesn't make you grateful. Do you know what it does do? It leaves you stuck right where you are, exhausted with what you have and filled with misery with those of like minds. We attract who and what we believe we deserve.

Don't forget to enjoy the beautiful journey of life. We are in charge of our thoughts, intentions, and actions. MY BLESSINGS ABUNDANTLY MANIFEST when I speak and think gratitude into my life.

Do you think we are a society that is always conditioned to want more? When is it enough for us to be happy? When will we feel complete with what we already have?

When we fail to be grateful, we give away our power to be happy and whole. I want to live a life where I focus on thanking the day.

I am grateful for the luck as well as the loss. I am thankful for the bumps and the triumphs. I am grateful for all the pain and my gains. Without the bad, the good wouldn't feel so amazing. So what are you grateful for?

I AM GROWING

You can't grow and stay the same... at the same time.

People won't admit this, but when you begin to grow, it makes other people uncomfortable and sometimes insecure when you start to level up and grow. So they begin to ask themselves, Where am I now in the pecking order of friendship? They have to ask themselves, why am I not where I want to be? When did I settle? The answer, almost every time, is you either didn't dream big enough, or you stopped dreaming altogether. And let me tell you, no one likes to realize that. I've been there. And when we can't celebrate someone else's success because of our stagnation, that speaks volumes to our growth and character.

How many people still look at you as a kid? As the person you were when you first met all those years ago? You know who they are- the parents, teachers, and bosses from your past. In their minds, people like you to stay small, literally, and figuratively because it gives them power over you, over knowing who you are. But the only constant thing is growth, and as we evolve, people don't like that; they fight you to stay the same. So people slowly begin to fall to the side and out of your life as you grow. But why?

For a long time, people still looked at me as a kid. Mind you; this was after I was all grown up. There is still a wide-eyed innocence, naivete, and purity within me. It equates to my youthfulness. I found there were times when my energy was too much for others.

Nonetheless, I began shrinking in rooms, dimming my light, even my physical being, to become accepted by societal standards. I began shrinking in rooms by becoming quieter and more subdued. I was worried that someone might think I was trying to diminish theirs by sharing my light. I didn't realize that my being made them feel less than, but that wasn't my fault or my problem; it was theirs.

I have been misinterpreted my whole life. My passion was seen as anger, my silliness mistaken for immaturity, my vulnerability was thought of as a weakness. I am light. There is still a wide-eyed naivete about certain things in the world because of how I discover. I like to observe; make people almost forget I am there to behave as authentically as possible. I used to fade into the background, to my detriment. In the back of my mind, I always wanted to rise and grow, feeling stifled in the structure of adulting.

I lost so many blessings because I refused to step into that power and strength that lies within me. Not wanting to be seen as a problem, I stifled my feelings and shrank and shrank. It wasn't until I lost a job that I finally had to address why. I thought I was being given a gift instead of realizing that I was the gift. Immediately, I began to expand. I took up space. After that happened, I swore never to shrink or make myself less than again.

Almost immediately, I began to play mothers. The roles of low vibration characters, such as drug addicts, divas, and drama, gave way to comedies and roles with a higher purpose. That was a defining time because I realized that I had grown more grounded, and others noticed it, too. I stopped shrinking. As an artist, I started asking directors and actors the hard questions, and I stood up for what I thought rang authentic for storytelling. As a woman, I stopped allowing others who did not acknowledge nor respect me into my energy.

I began to stretch so far that I thought I would snap. And that is the time I shot up like a bean sprout. I became light. I spoke up for myself and advocated for others. I made my presence unmistakable and my aura undeniable. I closed doors and walked away from situations, with class and grace, that no longer served me. That's what growth looks like. Never stop stretching.

I AM HAPPY

I smile in anger to keep calm and receptive.

Do you want to know the trick to happiness? Be present. Nine times out of ten, what's going on right now in your life, the very moment you are reading this, is okay.

Stop and survey your life and surroundings. Are you alive? Yes. Do you have the ability to be better than you were yesterday? Yes.

Happiness is a learned trait. Think about a baby. They take their visual cues from you. They learn to express themselves from your face. Let happiness come into your life and spread contagiously.

So, what makes us happy? What makes us happy is defined by what we have given the power to affect our mood. It's that simple and complicated. Lacking anything will leave you feeling unhappy. Living abundantly is the cure for happiness.

We must remind ourselves to enjoy the moment. Stop living in our past glories and failures and nervous about our unknown futures. Celebrate the wins, no matter how small.

I will tell a person real quick not to ask me to smile; that's a personal choice and one I leave for you to decide. But, when we are happy, we vibrate and congregate with like-minded people. I prefer to stand in a higher vibration because more good gets attracted to me. Nobody ever said their life was better by being surrounded by chronically pessimistic people. So be an emotional blessing and gift.

How can I make you happy and stay true to me? I can't. It's not my job to make anyone happy but me. No one but me is responsible for my happiness, as well. Yes, I can make other people's life feel nurtured, seen, and safe, but happy? No.

There will be times when things on the outside look fantastic, while there is turmoil and anguish on the inside. It's okay to visit there too. Just don't unpack that suitcase for an extended stay because you have a right to be and feel happy in this physical vacation called life. Enjoy your journey.

I AM HEALTHY

Health over wealth always.

When I was younger, I could eat anything I wanted and stay as skinny as a toothpick, and then the pandemic happened, and I gained a lot of weight. I felt it, y'all, my clothes no longer fit, and I couldn't ignore it anymore.

Stress, replaying the same day every day with an indoor life of tv and puzzles, and day drinking had taken over my body. This physical and mental vacation, as I tried to think of it at the time, had extended way past when it should have.

I was stress cooking and eating. I didn't realize how often I was eating as jeans gave way to athleisure wear and heels were turned in for sandals. I couldn't fit most of my clothes or shoes when it was time to go back to work. I needed a reset.

I wasn't doing my health and fitness routines. Mentally, I was on autopilot. This pandemic had completely messed up my mental health.

I stopped buying junk food, switched carbs for veggies and wine for water. I put down most of the junk food and quick meals. I took three-mile walks a day and started gentle stretching and yoga. Next, I did healthy meal kit deliveries for recipe ideas. Finally, I laid out in the sun for thirty minutes a day while listening to meditation music.

When I learned to live an all-around healthy life, the world around me began to change because I changed. Healthy living allows me to feel light in my spirit, which translates to my choices in terms of the food I eat, the thoughts I have, the words I speak, and the actions I take. Healthy living starts inside out. I became mindful of what I consumed in my body, from technology to other people's opinions.

Be mindful of the technology you consume, too. There is specific programming that can be unhealthy. I monitor my news and social media consumption; I walk away from gossip and listen to a lot of beautiful music. Regulate your mental health. Choosing things, people, and activities in the best general interest of my health is the best thing I can do for myself. This is the only vessel I get in this lifetime, so using or abusing it makes a difference.

So, I'll give you the same pep talk I gave myself. Whatever you're doing to make yourself feel lethargic and look unhealthy, stop! Be mindful of your harmful thoughts, unhealthy people, and unhealthy habits. You can choose to eat healthily. You can choose to exercise. You can choose a scoop of ice cream and not the whole container. A glass of wine will be fine, maybe not every night. A quick meal will be fine, but maybe only once a week. You don't need to deprive yourself of everything that you love. All you need is moderation. Take your vitamins, drink lots of water and oh yeah, cut yourself some slack. Stress keeps the weight on, too.

I AM HONEST

Telling my truth is telling the truth.

I am and have always been a terrible liar. My eyes tell what my mouth is too kind to say. I'm blunt and honest. I believe that lies hurt worse than the truth and that the truth will always come to the surface anyway. The lies we tell ourselves about how we feel can be so painful that we become physically ill from the mental and emotional anguish it takes on our spirits to lie and hide. How many of you have gotten headaches and stomach aches when you lied or could feel when someone you trusted was lying to you?

Lies take a toll on all our relationships, especially with ourselves. If you can't trust yourself because you know, how can you trust and believe others? Lying leads to overthinking and overexplaining.

Authentic talk can go on for hours and allow people with similar and different views the opportunity to learn and appreciate the viewpoints of another. I would never want to cheat myself or others of real connection. Human connection is the reason we live a 3D existence.

People say there is no "your truth"; there is only "the truth." The truth is your truth can be the truth. We are either honest, or we are dishonest.

However, I am allowed to change my mind, opinion, and actions after a good honest conversation. That doesn't make me dishonest; it makes me evolve. Remember that. It means we now, after evaluation and contemplation, believe something else. And guess what? That's okay. You can change your mind from what you once thought to something else and still stand in truth.

Here's the hard part about honesty; some people are not and never will be ready to hear or speak the truth. Use discernment, please. Know that as you speak your truth, which is the truth as you see it, you will lose those you have loved along the way. Everyone is not ready for this level of reality. Some are content to sit and stay in the land of what they want to see. Sometimes you have to leave them there to sit and stay right where they are, living a lie.

I AM HUMBLE

If I have to tell you how kind I am, repeatedly, I'm probably lying.

Did you see who I dedicated this book to? The meek; the humble. Y'all, the meek are getting ready to inherit the Earth. We are tired of watching the people in power abuse it. Watch the news, you'll see. People are going to jail and losing jobs for abuse of power. No more. That energy will no longer be tolerated.

I didn't grow up with a lot. I struggled for decades to pay my bills. Then one day, I could pay off my student loans, open a savings account and move out of my crappy apartment.

I watched people go from not acknowledging my existence to going out of their way to open doors. Did I change? No, not really. All money and power do is amplify who you are. If anything, I went more within myself.

I became aware of the climb instead of the grind. I moved slowly, figuring out how I wanted to use my purpose for good and influence positive change. I thanked those who allowed me to journey quietly and stayed by my side. Then one day, I thought, Universe, you have blessed me with so much. How can I give back? How can I finally feel safe to open up and share your gifts? This book is that first step. I'm giving you tools that can help you move humbly up the ranks and into your power and destiny.

Why did it have to happen this way? Because no one listens unless you create a platform. For years, I shared the secrets of manifestation and purpose planning. Still, few listened because, in their eyes, I wasn't living the life of abundance. One night, I looked up at the stars, completely down, with barely a nickel to my name, and uttered these two words to the moon: I'm ready. Nine months later, it's like I birthed a new life. People started to listen.

So many people are used to working on other people's platforms and for other people's agendas. So who do you think writes the speeches? Who do you believe schedules and runs the meetings? The humble, but that didn't matter, so I had to learn a new way to show humility.

Never once brag about what you have. As quickly as you receive it, you can lose it. Remember who you were before the climb. Take someone up the ladder with you; they will help keep you grounded. Mentor someone who needs to know how you do what you do. The jump will seem less scary for them. Help those who are less fortunate. If you're only on this Earth to help yourself, you can only go so far, and if you do go far, when you fall, there will be no one to catch you because you moved through life selfishly.

Why is the humble going to inherit the Earth? We move stealthily up the ranks. You are beginning to see many people in power who would not have been in power years earlier. We push through painful childhoods and circumstances that are meant to keep us at the bottom, but we find people with common agendas, and as a group, we rise. The humble don't try to impress; they only want to bless.

People confuse meek with weak. That's when they underestimate the strength of humility: rise and lead.

I AM KIND

The true test of kindness is when you're down.

Do not let a problematic heart harden your kind mind. When we attempt to prove a point and show the truth, we sometimes forget to be kind. We forget that it's not most important to be right but to create a safe space to feel understood and understand others. Never allow anyone with a cruel intention, action, or word to ruin your kind mind and heart. Never.

How can I be more kind? It's a question I ask myself when I feel like I'm seconds away from exploding. I get still and try harder than ever to listen, not just to the words spoken but also the emotion behind the words. It's not about me. If I make it about me, I miss the message and ignore the messenger. If I'm angry, how much of this anger is because of what transpired between us and how much came way before me? I attempt to reach out, touch, connect.

And if all else fails, I walk away before saying something that I cannot take back.

Kindness changes the way that we see ourselves and treat others. It is staring into the eyes of another with openness and light. That's a terrifying place to go to for people because kindness involves a level of vulnerability that some may not have earned.

Suppose we can get through the hurdles of fear. In that case, kindness moves us into a place of greater compassion, confidence, helpfulness, and control. Empathy makes us more generous people with our time, things, and words. It brings out the optimism in us. Kindness makes us more understanding; we become more proactive than reactive.

CHECK IN #2

I'm learning that it's easier to advise than to receive it. I'm learning that starting inward and figuring out how to feel good about myself will trickle over to the external. I'm learning that you have to do the work. You can't talk about what you want; take action as well. I am learning to change and growth.

I'm learning that writing exposes my flaws while highlighting my humanity. I'm learning that I'm okay with sharing those flaws. I'm learning how much of an introvert I have become. I'm learning that being an introvert doesn't necessarily mean that you are quiet; it means you recharge better alone.

I'm learning to step out of the box, my comfort zone, and do and say things that scare me. I'm learning to release the inner child and let her heal. I'm learning that love is all about free will. I'm learning that I require trust, respect, open and honest communication in all relationships more than love.

The pay-off is so great. But most importantly, I'm learning that my words affect change, not just in myself but in others. My words are valued, respected, and well-received.

Oh yeah... and check up on my family and friends.

I AM LEARNING

Involve me so I learn.

Not everybody and everything is for you. The people you spend the most time with show you who you are. They are your past, present, and potentially your future. Whatever isn't healed will eventually be revealed. I've thought a lot about that knowledge over the years and hit my head several times trying to save, help or heal people that were unwilling to do so for themselves.

People typically learn three ways: seeing, hearing, or doing. We expect to read, hear, or see something, then begin to embody the concept. That's not how my brain works. I have always been pretty kinesthetic. It would be best if you involved me. I kept putting myself in situations, on repeat, until I stopped the enabling behavior. I had a lot to unlearn.

Why do life's biggest lessons always seem to stick after you experience them? Do you realize how hard it is to unlearn what has been ingrained in your childhood? Conflict resolution, financial responsibility, and self-care were not big staples in my family. I had to go to therapy.

This moment is the first time in this book that I have talked about therapy and its importance in my life. Therapy taught me to UNLEARN everything I was taught to be true. If you love someone hard enough, they will change for the better. Family is blood only. I can't be, do or have certain things because of my current circumstances—all lies. I had never known myself more and realized I had no clue who I was when I first started therapy. The emotional intelligence and vulnerability required were not anything I had experienced growing up.

Therapy taught me how to heal and help. Involve me in the process, don't print me off a checklist. Education starts with teaching one person the tools they need to thrive, not survive, and once illuminated, shared with others.

What will you teach me today, Universe? You are to set goals and speak positively about yourself, affirm your value and worth as a person, share your knowledge, challenges, and growth. You allowed yourself to fall but got back up. Victims don't become victorious in life, only warriors. And to be a warrior, you must be the student, the obstacle, and the teacher in life. So I hear you, Universe, and thank you.

I AM LOGICAL

Logic for good, heals. Logic for bad, harms.

My name is Maya Lynne. For the past two decades, I do not introduce myself as Maya or Yaya or any other name. I do go by ML, as well. Some people have known me throughout my life and have addressed me by these names. I have asked all to call me Maya Lynne out of respect for me. I cannot tell you how many people ignore it, "forget," or laugh it off. Okay, time to put me in their shoes. Out of my heart and into my head, I say.

As a pretty emotional person, I have to come at this from a logical point of view. People want to feel connected to me and that is why they call me by whatever name they are comfortable/familiar with. I understand that. That's a very logical argument.

But what about my comfort? What about my respect? No, I correct them and if they continue to ignore my request, I limit communication. Logic also means paying attention to the reasons why people put rules and boundaries into place. Logic helps validate someone's truth.

Sitting down and explaining why I prefer and only respond to Maya Lynne exhausted me. I was wasting my breath. And then, the answer came. Logic demands that enforcing boundaries is good. Just don't respond to the repeat offenders. When asked why I don't respond, I tell others that it's not my name unless they say - Maya Lynne. We cannot ignore direct eye contact, a calm demeanor, and killer logic.

Is that extreme? Yes. Is it logical? Yes. Logic is a reasonable way of thinking. So, for example, suppose a situation or person is causing me discomfort or disrespect. In that case, the logical thing to do is limit connection with what hurts/harms me.

I've learned to differentiate what I feel from what I think. One thing that needs to be done when I'm in a disagreement is to keep clear and calm. It's the only way to reason and to reach me. Just because the way a person communicates in conflict makes them comfortable doesn't mean it makes me comfortable. Reasoning requires listening and understanding while taking the emotion out of the situation to keep the facts.

How can we work from a more logical point of view? First, listen. Logic keeps your feelings from getting hurt once you understand where someone else is coming from, even if they don't know where you are coming from. The head makes a choice that appears to be heart-based, but it's mental clarity in reality.

The mind is mighty. Once I mastered hearing others' responses to my thoughts, feeling, and needs, I learned how to promote understanding, compromise, and master logic in difficult conversations. Ultimately, a rational mind taught me to protect my space and be open to healing connections.

I AM LOVING

Love is being seen, nurtured, and safe.

Love is patience. Love is kind. It's not just about how you love someone else; it's also about how you love yourself. You have to be the love you want. Self-love comes first. Love's foundation starts with self. You can't love someone else until you love yourself. You can't love yourself until you define love.

Don't just tell me what love is; show me. Teach me through your actions and deeds. Teach me without fear or expecting anything in return and give foolishly. I have wrestled with a lot of conditional love over and over again. There are those only willing to be in my life and show love to me if I behave, talk, or think a certain way. When I speak my mind, and my thoughts are not aligned with theirs, folks disappear. It is a haunt from childhood that plagued me long into my adult years and caused severe self-esteem and abandonment issues.

We get so used to conditional love that if someone doesn't do as we require, we walk away from those relationships that moments earlier were so valuable and essential. Therapy taught me that rejection is my protection in a new direction.

We use love, or the thought of it, to control who we allow in our lives and how we will enable them to show up. Yeah, you read that right. We use love as manipulation. Love is not meant to be used; it is not a tool but a virtue.

Love has become about where we can get it instead of giving it. Don't chase love; attract it. Anything meant for you to love will magnetically come to you.

We live in a society that is crying out for authentic connection. It is our birthright and a reason the 3D world exists. We are deserving of all the handshakes, kisses, cuddles, and smiles we want. We are worthy of all the hugs and laughter that relationships bring. My love is all-encompassing and raw.

Even on my worst days, I love. It may have to be from afar, but I show up in a frank and private way. Text message check-ins, random phone calls, and video chats are not necessarily on display for the world to see. But to the people who matter, they know, and that's what matters.

Be gentler with yourself. Show yourself grace and patience when you're unsure what the next step is. Allow pampering to occur because there is healing power in taking wellness days for self-love.

And let's not forget that love is pain. Breaking away from people and things that hurt you instead of healing you can be devastating. Love breaks your heart, mends, but can grow back even more potent. Love never stops. You are the love that you seek. Never stop loving.

I AM LOYAL

I'd rather have an old sweatshirt that still fits and feels good than a new one that's ill-fitting and stiff.

I am a faithful and steadfast friend and family member. When others look at the people in my tribe with judgment or disregard, I do not engage.

I have never understood why it is so important to fit in instead of standing out. Fit in and watch people act like jerks or stand up for the ones you love. How is that a hard decision?

People get treated like pennies. Shiny today, spent and forgotten tomorrow. No matter what privilege and socio-economic status say, No one person is more valuable than another.

There were, are, and will be times when your values, beliefs, and life align more with others; therefore, more communication will occur. But please understand that's what it is.

My best friend and I could not have more different lives. I have no idea what she does during the day, and she had no idea what I do. But we value the longevity, the secrets, the honest, open, and safe communication that only our decades of shorthand conversation would understand. There are no secrets or lies. There are no sides to take. There are differing opinions where we agree to disagree. And if we need a break, we take it. I got so mad at her once I didn't talk to her for seven months. But you know what I didn't do? Talk bad behind her back and that's loyalty.

Speak from your place of pain openly and honestly. NEVER allow another person to come between you and the bond you feel for those closest to you. Hold each other accountable for our actions and words privately. The world doesn't need to know y'all got beef, pork, chicken, or shrimp with other people.

When you get to be there for someone's scariest moments and enjoy quiet and great conversations full of laughter, you recognize and appreciate the layers of loyalty in your relationships.

Who am I loyal to and why? First and foremost, myself. If I feel I am abandoning my authentic essence, I regroup. Who is faithful to me? Sometimes it feels like a revolving door with a handful of constant day ones. Treat me publicly and privately - with respect, trust, honesty, love, and communication. Show someone you care. Everyone deserves to feel at home with someone.

I AM MATURE

Maturity is a mindset not an age.

You can be 50 and still the most immature person in the world. Maturity is a mindset, not an age. It is the ability to decipher problems and make conscious and critical decisions on handling something with wisdom and decorum.

I cannot tell you how to be mature. The choices we make in dealing with our trauma directly correlate with how we respond to criticisms, consequences, and the unknown. It's easy to feign maturity when you are getting what you want. But what if you're not? What if the way you want things is not beneficial for the greater good of everyone? Do you have people bend towards your will or do you compromise? That's grown people's status right there. It's realizing that your way might not always be best and willing to listen and learn and not just talk and tell.

Just because we pay taxes, buy homes, and plan for retirement, doesn't mean we're mature. Maturity is not just a mental state of being; it is also a deed. Taking physical, mental, emotional, and financial responsibility for your actions or lack thereof is important. Holding yourself accountable for how you got to this present space and what you allowed in your life will tell you everything you need to know about maturity.

Other people are entitled to know things and express their feelings in a physically, emotionally, and mentally safe space. You may not know everything, so put yourself in rooms where others can teach you. And the way you receive and give, in that energy, displays the ultimate maturity.

I AM OPEN

If there is something better than I know, teach me.

The search. I love searching for the truth. None of us have all the answers, so there's always something to investigate and someone to help us.

Something that I talk about a lot is the light in the eyes. As the eyes are the windows to the soul, we can see and share all the fears and vulnerabilities by looking within each other and ourselves. We share our joys and excitement, too.

What stops us from being open? Fear of being wrong or being misunderstood. We only want to appear our best in front of others. Openness requires the ability to showcase our flaws.

That doesn't mean you should share everything you're thinking and feeling because everyone is not thinking and feeling in your best interest. What I mean is every day does not have to be rainbows and roses. Sometimes, days can be the rain and the thorns, and that's okay. You will find your soul tribe through the trials.

When we nurture our development and evolution, we know we strengthen our belief in ourselves. It forces us to look at what we value as important or "right."

I AM PEACE

The place of peace lives inside of us, not outside.

I find peace in a place where there is nothing. No sound, but the wind. No friend, but the trees. No view, but the sky. I love the quiet and the calm. There is fresh air, usually in the early morning. I can hear my thoughts there. That is my place of peace.

Peace can also be a mental space. I am at peace when living present in my thoughts, feelings, and actions. So, here's an exercise. Take a moment and assess your surroundings. Wherever you are right now, take three cleansing breaths. Then, relax your shoulders and ask yourself, Am I okay? Listen to your mind, heart, and body response. If tension arises, you may not be present, positive, or peace-filled.

We're only really breathing well out of one nostril at a time. If you're breathing out your right nostril, your mind is more active. If you're breathing out of your left nostril, your mind is calmer. Breathe until you feel the airflow free through that left nostril. I promise you will feel the difference.

We are at peace when we unapologetically exist. We are at peace when we don't take on other people's problems as our own.

Find peace by listening to your voice and intuition. Acknowledge that your thoughts and feelings have value; they matter. You matter. You are enough. You are right where you are supposed to be. It's a state of being. Meditation, yoga, even sitting quietly and listening to your breath, your vibration commands peace.

Do not allow anyone to steal your peace, manipulate it or undermine its necessity in your life. We all deserve the right to feel calm, safe, present, and centered. Slow down and enjoy life's moments—no need to rush through living.

I AM POWERFUL

Be so strong you break the chains you created.

Power is not given; it is taken. Being powerful is being yourself no matter what other people tell you they are comfortable with you being.

As an African American woman, I have been told that the passion in my voice is interpreted as anger. My boldness is bossy. My light and energy are "too much." My response? You're welcome.

You want to be well-received, but we've made power a bad thing. Power doesn't change who you are; it just highlights who you were all along. Power reveals your character. People have a subjective choice in how they see me. If my passion makes you uncomfortable, that's not a reflection of me; it's a reflection of you.

I believe so strongly in myself that others have no choice but to believe in me. My inner power is stronger than any outside force. I can change, create and illuminate anything I want.

You must hone your power to prosper. Words affect change because words are powerful. Some may not like to give words the credit they deserve due to no physical damage. Still, the mental damage that words can create affects us physically, emotionally, mentally, and spiritually. This trickles back to childhood y'all. No more. Take your power back. Healing is power

Words spoken are as powerful as thoughts. Thoughts become words that fuel actions. And when our words do not grant us the power to move in a powerful direction, change them, or they will change you.

I AM PRACTICAL

I am realistic. I expect miracles.

Society has often looked for ways to do something different or flashy instead of what may be best or safest. Do you know what not being practical does? It leaves you broke. Your spirit, bank account, and reality depleted because you tried to keep up appearances that weren't emotionally or financially sensible.

There is an importance to dreaming big, planning for the life you want, and figuring out that there will be risks that you need to take to get what you want. But this "fake it until you make it" mentality is exactly what I'm talking about. You are not living and acknowledging your actual reality. For decades, I had nothing. Budgeting became very important to make ends meet. As my budget increased, so did my expenses, but could I continue to live the way I had when I had less? Yes. I had chosen to improve my lifestyle as my budget increased.

I try to look at the bright side of dull practicality. I can live my life comfortably for years to come, give to charities, help my family and sleep peacefully.

My practical side gets my deadlines done, my bills paid on time, and my home organized. Ain't nothing wrong with that. I live with what I need and some of what I want and stay smart about how much I share. So, I glow in silence. That's real.

I AM PRESENT

Let the past stay right where it is and the future left unknown.

Every time you bring something from the past, you give power to it instead of focusing on the present, which now has no room. I notice that when people live in the past, those were the glory days. The high school football quarterback or the student council president can be stories told repeatedly where you are throwing the game-winning catch or staging a student revolt for change. It almost feels like you can't allow yourself to look at where you are now because it doesn't compare to what was, but please remember you can't go back to yesterday. Living in the past is almost like believing the best has already passed you by.

On the flip side, worrying about the future can feel like you're nervous you won't get there, to whatever goal you have. The present is a truly magical place. It is the ability to manifest what you want and consciously choose to make it happen. Knowing that the past is guaranteed has a significant impact on the present. The present should give hope for the future instead of depression focused on history.

When I am present, I know I give to my blessings and my challenges. This book is a perfect example. Do you know I've been trying to write this book for almost six years? I could have just said, well, I've done all of these other amazing things, and this book isn't unfolding as I want, so let me shelve it forever. I could also say I don't know what the future holds, and maybe being an author isn't meant for me. But instead, I started again—many times.

What held me back was not feeling like I had accomplished enough in the past to be credible. One day, I stopped focusing on the past as if it were the present. It just clicked. These are my feelings and thoughts. What credentials do I need to share? Um, life experience.

I took some of my past writings, added in some future manifestations and present thoughts, and boom, there is a book. And you are reading this book. I couldn't write this book until I affirmed myself. I had to be present, at a place of strength and growth. You can't authentically write down what you don't feel.

I smile because I know that I am no longer living in the past as I type this. The problems and the glories of the past don't define me any longer.

Also, if I had written it before now, some of this knowledge would not be here. For example, suppose I had waited for someone to read it and validate my experiences before sending it to the publisher. In that case, I might have doubted what was meant to affirm. So, please stop talking about what you did or what you're going to do and do it now. You might enjoy the moment.

I AM PROGRESS

Progress is impossible without compromise.

I know that to become progress, I have to know what I want and where I want to go in life. You cannot make progress until you find and follow your goals.

You know those moments when you feel anxious about not knowing what's next or exhausted because you feel like you're throwing everything at the wall to see what sticks? That's because you are not living in your purpose. Your path involves passion, service, and purpose. So I had to ask myself, what am I passionate about? What are the things that don't feel like work? Usually, we turn these things into our vocation.

How can you help others? In what ways can you give back? That's your service. It has to involve helping someone other than yourself to better all humanity.

What is your purpose? That's where people get stuck because there is an aspect of ambition that people do not want to address; what we need to improve. There is nothing that fulfills us more than improving something that challenges us. The things that we are talented in can propel us to progress in life. What you are passionate about is just as important.

Hopefully, I'm unlocking something in you. You will either realize that you have been stagnant and complacent in your life, or you are genuinely progressing to fulfill your purpose. Don't be afraid to dream big. If you've already reached your goal, make a new one. Never stop being willing to learn and progress in multiple areas of your life. I encourage you to go after what you want in life. It will show up when you have prepared and when you need it. Never give up.

I AM RELAXED

Sleep and eat for the best retreat.

Who or what makes you feel relaxed? I am calm when getting a massage, a pedicure, or sleeping. When there are pockets of time that I can sit and breathe, and I know I've done the things for the day on my checklist, I am relaxed. But, to me, there is nothing more relaxing than knowing that everything on my to-do list has been done.

I grew up with a strong work ethic, preparing meals for myself and ensuring my homework was done. I was taught if you're not doing something, you're doing nothing. It was meant to teach me to be proactive in my growth and development as a person, but what it taught me was always to stay chaotically busy.

I would get anxious if there weren't something I had to do or somewhere I had to go. One day, a friend took me outside and practiced guided meditation with me. I didn't take to it like a fish to water, but I did take to the nature aspect. It was about not clearing my mind but choosing the sights, sounds, and smells I wanted to focus on and not taking on everything at once.

After months of practice, I was finally getting into the practice of meditation and its health benefits, including relaxation. My mind and my muscles calm. I learned that ease does not mean silencing all the thoughts in your head; it's about choosing which ones to focus on for that moment.

Write a list. Write a list of everything you need to get done. Then, knock everything off until you have it narrowed down to the three most important things for that day. Anything more, and nothing ever really gets completed. Finally, finish it off with something nice for yourself. A bath, an hour of tv, or playing a game with your kids. Because honestly, we only feel like we are relaxing when we get lost in time. Enjoy those moments.

CHECK IN #3

I'm learning the importance of editing. I can see the flaws in my communication and work on improving them. I'm learning that all of life's lessons are for this moment. I was meant to write this book at this moment. I'm learning that there is no wrong way to tell your story if it is infused with honesty, love, and an uplifting message.

I'm learning the skill it takes to be disciplined. Writing, rewriting, and reorganizing your thoughts for long periods is not for the weak-minded but for the successful. I'm learning the importance of completion.

As I am three-quarters of the way through this book, I finally begin to see the finish line. I am learning that progress comes from courage. Everybody isn't going to like, understand or agree with what I am saying and that's fine with me. We all have free will.

I am learning that this book is a purge, releasing what no longer serves my ego. I am learning to find my rhythm and voice as an author and truly see myself as an essential voice. I'm learning to love all the hard work.

I AM RESPECTFUL

You either go or grow from my life.

You cannot expect to talk or treat someone any old kind of way that you want and have them treat you nicely in return. So, for me, learning how to take responsibility for how and what I say has been the greatest gift. It doesn't matter what the intention is if the execution is half-assed, lackluster, or ill-received.

What are some ways that I show respect? The most significant form of care is learning my name and when to use it. I use this example often. I call ma'am, sir, or speak to anyone twenty years older than me with the etiquette of respect. Anyone twenty years or younger than me, I ask you to call me Miss Maya Lynne. Children love to call me Momma Maya Lynne. With my age comes knowledge and demands respect.

What happened to saying please and thank you? When did we become so casual that we speak familiarity with people we don't even know well? I'm not saying that everyone should behave this way; ask your elder how they would like to be addressed. Take the extra step to formalize communication until you are in a familiar enough space to engage otherwise. Remember always to speak and treat others as you expect them to speak and treat you.

Everyone is not your equal. Everyone is also not your subordinate either. We should expect humanity to treat us with respect, regardless of gender, race, sexual orientation, socioeconomic situation, or creed.

I AM RESPONSIBLE

I build decisions for long-term visions.

I miss being a kid. Summer vacation, no taxes, and riding bikes until dark feels so long ago. Now, being a full-fledged adult, nothing happens in my life that I do not have control over, whether it's my decisions or my response.

I don't ever have just one source of income. If one source fails, there is always something else to lift me.

Eat well, drink plenty of water, work smart, pay taxes, love hard, be willing to be wrong, and every once in a while, let that inner child go outside and ride a bike until dark. This affirmation is self-explanatory. You know what you're supposed to do and what you've got to do to accomplish it.

I AM SENSUAL

Make passion an experience.

Either people are afraid to talk about passion or are so open I'm like, do you have a filter? Ha! Sensuality is a hot-button topic because most people equate it to only sex. It's much more than that. So there is touch, taste, smell, and what you hear and see. That's right; it's all your senses.

I don't ever talk about sex publicly, but it's essential to know and express what turns you on. Open up your imagination. Think about your fantasies and talk about them with your loved one. Be positive and not critical about what you like or don't like.

Number one rule, when in doubt, start and go slow until you're both comfortable talking about or doing anything. It's human nature. Hold space for your partner to feel vulnerable enough to share their desires and receive your pleasures. Talking about your fantasies and desires with anyone can be extremely hard because a level of trust and vulnerability is required.

Make sure you both feel incredibly safe in word and deed. Be clear if something is happening that you don't want to. People have different boundaries. It's important to create a safe space when talking about intimacy. It's such a vulnerable act and conversation.

I AM SINCERE

Public and private behavior should align. Don't be fake.

People can read energy very well. It's a three levels deep version of genuine. You know when you feel it. The moment you look at your partner or friend, and there is a truly natural sense of joy in their eyes for your happiness, that's sincerity. The concern you see in someone's eyes and hear in their voice as they worry about your heart or your health.

Sincerity is a pretty fantastic gift. It's the difference between friend and friendly. It's what separates the always people from the right now ones.

When you find people who will tell you how they feel in the most loving and open of ways, hold on to them.

I AM SPIRITUAL.

Spirituality dictates my faith, not religion.

Meditation is my teacher and yoga is my prayer. I seek healing from nature and fellowship from soul sessions with friends. My spirit recharges from solitude and silence, and I believe in something greater than me. These are all things that I do to get closer to myself, my purpose, and the Universe. I no longer allow anyone to destroy my peace.

Being spiritual can be challenging for some who enjoy the fellowship of religion and thrive from the mutual energy of congregational growth. However, whatever spiritual path you choose, make sure your beliefs align with healing, high vibrations, and peace.

Our spirits live on long after our bodies do. This is a 3D world, and we are here to learn, grow and connect on a deeper level than that of the flesh. Talking to each other's souls should be a major goal.

Make sure to give yourself guidance and grace. And fill it with purpose.

I AM SUCCESS

To finish anything lifts the spirit and discourages laziness.

What goals have I yet to accomplish, and how will I make it happen? Those are the first questions I ask myself when I get into a real groove, plotting how to live successfully in life.

Have you ever gotten exactly what you wanted, became extremely happy, and then... the blues? It's that thought of, "Now what?" Well, that's because your measurement of success was so small that you saw the mini victory as the grand prize. Either that or you made it to your goal and didn't have another benchmark for yourself on how to continue your success.

Mostly, and this may be hard to acknowledge, you either did not dream big enough, or you stopped creating growth (goals) for yourself. I have been guilty of all of the above. I had to unlearn everything I knew about success. It's a mindset of when confidence, opportunity, and discipline collide. I had to learn to dream big and believe I could have anything if I worked hard enough.

I used to have a hard time finishing goals because I didn't know what was next. Success comes when you fight past the fear of change and the unknown. It requires growing, learning, and implementing.

Success comes when you give up the highs and lows of your past. The past made you but does not have to define you now.

When I cross something off my list to get to the ultimate big goal, there is a success. When I stop trying to add more things to do in a day and focus on the three most important to progress me and my dreams, there is a success. When I say no to something that doesn't fuel my mind, body, or soul because it does not align with my vibration, goals, or dreams, I also feel successful.

Be fueled by all your accomplishments. That's the best way to measure success.

I AM THRIVING

Don't fail, flourish haphazardly.

If the light that shines in me and through me causes you to feel blinded instead of illuminated, that says everything about your character, not mine. I will not snuff my accomplishments to uplift yours, and I shouldn't have to. I have thrived in the face of adversity and adversaries.

I grew up knowing that I didn't have a choice but to work harder than I did the day before to get the life I wanted. Getting good grades and going to college were all I could think about. So I took some pretty giant leaps to feel like I'm thriving finally.

Thriving is the significant step I took that has led me to my higher vibrational self. When I look back, I see how far I've come, and when I look forward, I see the unknown of where I'm heading. The higher I climb, the brighter the light, the clearer the journey, and I fear less.

It reminds me that I survived something that I overcame and bloomed from, whether it was an external or internal obstacle.

Congratulations on making it through that valley to rise high on the peak! Once you get there, you know you never want to fall so hard again, so you continue to better yourself and keep rising. Learning to implement healthy boundaries is the difference between short-term and long-term prosperity.

People thrive together. No one can do it alone forever and sustain. You must trust others to vibe up with you, take some of the weight off your shoulders, celebrate your victories, tell you the truth even when it hurts, and hold you accountable.

If you don't feel like you're thriving, find a mentor. Find someone doing what you want to do or who can help you brainstorm the plan. Then stop procrastinating and making excuses about timing and do the work. Thriving is in your hands.

I AM TRIUMPHANT

Don't mistake stillness for being still. I'm a beast.

One of the best feelings in the world is grinding hard privately and then exploding publicly with all you have accomplished. Completion. Don't let people fool you into thinking that celebrating your accomplishments is the same as bragging. It's not. That's their ego, not yours.

In all honesty, being triumphant is about celebrating something you didn't think you could achieve. Against all those odds, you're still standing, more prominent, better, and brighter than before. It means you conquered something that wasn't easy. So give yourself the power to enjoy the outcome of the journey.

You showed up with strength and courage and overcame things that you or others thought you never could. Bravo!

I AM VALUABLE

Your words and opinions of me do not dictate my value.

I have something to say. I have something to share. The things I know and the life I have lived have value. So my value is not dictated by what other people think of me nor by my past actions or plans. I think of value as internal validation and worth as external.

What is valuable to me? Time is precious. We only have one life that we know about, and spending it on people who don't matter or don't value your time will drain you from the precious moments you could be spending with others. Tomorrow is not promised to anyone, so be mindful of who you stake your time in.

Where I have been, I can help others without going through it. Also, if someone is going through something, I've learned that it's possible to help them figure out how to get out of their circumstances by realizing that they are not alone. So suppose we have the information and ability to help. In that case, it is our responsibility to do what we can to share that knowledge.

When someone doesn't value you, please do not spend your time explaining who you are. Simply put, stand in the power of your character, ethics, and personal worth and leave others out of your intuition.

You are a prize, hold yourself in high esteem accordingly. You are gold.

I AM VERSATILE

I'm not shaped for boxes, so don't try to put me into one.

My skills and goals are as diverse as the wigs that I wear. They both take grooming, fearlessness, and creativity. Do you stand out or try to fit in?

It's important to know how to do a lot of things and how to do them well. Utility players on sports teams play more often because they can perform well doing multiple positions. Artists, actors, and other creatives have to be extremely versatile in order to work in different mediums successfully.

We live in a world that relies on our ability to be adaptable, whether it's through technology updates, scientific discoveries, etc. We are programmed to learn, understand and execute proficiently in order to stay knowledgeable and current.

I will be the first person to tell you that change makes my head want to explode, but the reason I push myself to stay versatile is because it allows me to address complex challenges. I am never bored. Versatility gives us the ability to stand out while building collective skills and relationships. Don't we all want that? To unite in our diversity?

Don't be afraid to do and know a little about a lot of things. You are a gift, chameleon.

I AM VULNERABLE

Vulnerability is braveness stepping in front of fear.

This lesson can be challenging because I like to put my best effort out there. What I am finding is the more I share my story, the more people relate to me. Sometimes, my vulnerability is also a turnoff because it makes others uncomfortable, or maybe they don't want to be expected to share, as well.

I was taught not to share what I know because people will use it against me to hurt me. I was also taught vulnerability takes away your power in relationships. I was taught that everyone leaves eventually, so don't share too much because they will turn your wounds into weapons.

I had to unlearn all that I was taught. Most of my relationships taught me, conditional love. I was shown love if I behaved a certain way, said what they wanted to hear, or did as they desired. If not, I was discarded.

This way of life is actually what lead me to my passion- acting. I can share and convey what I, Maya Lynne, was really thinking or feeling fearlessly and free of judgment through playing characters.

Ultimately, that is not a feeling that can be sustained over time. First, it wasn't healthy, and second, I wanted to turn it off. Lastly, it led me to therapy because when you grow up in a household being told that children should be seen and not heard, you learn to hide. So character should be a part of you, just not all of you.

Acting is all about vulnerability. It's the connection between two or more characters and what makes me care about and root for them. During the story, I believe everything I, as a character, am saying. Once cut is yelled, I bottled up that vulnerability back up.

The hardest thing to do in life is to be vulnerable. Sharing your feelings, questions, and concerns. When we feel the rejection, dismissal, or abuse from sharing that gift, it can cripple our ability to stay open. Yes, I chose to be an actor, knowing that this would be a big test for me.

Know this; it is okay to not talk about your feelings if you are not ready or a person who constantly ridicules and mocks your open heart. The important thing is that you find a community of people to share your feelings, whether a friend or a support group.

I can honestly say I didn't appreciate my journey to vulnerability until 2020. Life now feels more precious. Relationships and honesty are more transparent, and feelings and values are deeply felt.

Do not bottle your feelings inside or think that no one cares. It will only make you sick and even more paranoid. And be careful who you share your vulnerability with because not everybody cares about you who knows about you.

I AM WISE

Wisdom is learned not earned.

If you know everything, then whom are you learning from? Surround yourself with people you can teach and who can also teach you. You will never be foolish a day in your life.

Wisdom comes from books; it also comes from experiences and instincts. But, mostly, it comes from collaboration. To be wise is to know you don't know everything but that you have something to offer that can help yourself and others on the journey to purpose.

When we share wisdom, we can change people's lives. Take this book, for example. This book is all about understanding. It's a lot of things, my opinions, life lessons learned, and my desire to help other people so that maybe they don't have to go through the trials and tribulations that I did to manifest the best. Because the wisest people know that sharing knowledge is a service and a blessing to someone, be willing to be someone else's blessing with what you have learned. Each one teaches one.

I AM WORTHY

I place value on me not money.

By 2015, I was knocked down so many times in life that I began to think my life had no meaning. I felt worthless. Externally and internally, very little was going my way. I was stuck at the bottom of a big rotting hole. This is the one that I didn't want to write. This is the reason I wrote this book because I finally learned to embrace this message.

One day, in 2015, I had it all, everything I thought I wanted. Within six months, I became single, lost my job, totaled my car, and had my second miscarriage. I hit rock bottom. Worth is tough to explain; it's how I see the external, outside of me, challenges testing me. The greatest challenge the Universe has given me regarding worth is motherhood.

After two miscarriages, IVF fertility issues, polyps, and more, I began to wonder if I was worthy of a good life. Since 2015, the pain of miscarriages, breast cancer scares, eviction notices, abuse, racism, sexism, classism, car accidents, fake friends, users, abusers, manipulators, poverty, anxiety, and depression, to name a few, were enough bad breaks to kill some people. Unfortunately, I hadn't realized my strength yet. Most of that list was happening to me at the same time that year. It made me believe that this was my fate, my punishment from a previous life perhaps, that I didn't deserve a happily ever after. My worth was wrapped up in rejection and sadness while I continued to surround myself with people who used me. I was mistreated, expended, and on the brink of homelessness and allowed society to strip away my worth.

Yes, life got tough and I was alone more than I wanted or deserved. However, now, I am a homeowner and feel safe and secure in a way I never had before. My blessings have helped affirm my worth in ways that words still cannot.

I have finally conquered this attribute and made it my friend and not my foe. How? Maybe I haven't birthed children, and perhaps I never will, but the love and light that I have poured into other people's children have been just as important. I have healed my wounds and turned them into wisdom. I have released the desire to want to know what's coming next all the time. I have smiled as each new cycle begins, leaving behind someone or something that no longer serves my higher self. I have learned to head to new beginnings fearlessly. I have affirmed myself, my needs, and my wants. And being in therapy, too, never hurts.

I stopped looking to anyone outside of myself to validate my thoughts and feelings. I realized that what others offer me may not be of worth to me, and the only solution is to validate myself. I have finally begun to create the life I deserve by affirming who I am. Now is the time to let nature and nurture take their course.

I am looking forward to the continuous release of what no longer serves me.

I knew I was worthy
I knew I was somebody
Not just anybody

Or everybody

And everything that tried to tell me

I am

Unworthy

Would be proven wrong

Strong-will

Determination

Focus

I am a survivor

I am great at a lot of things

I always knew I would see my name in lights and on billboards

Because

I am good

I am deserving of recognition, respect, and opportunities

I am worthy

I am

I AM ZEALOUS

I root for everyone, even those who don't wish me well.

This may be the end of this book, but it's only the middle of my journey and the beginning of a whole new one. I am incredibly excited about what the world will throw my way as I continue to move through my purpose.

There will be challenging days of challenges, and I look forward to them just as much as the brighter ones. Welcoming today with wide-eyed wonderment and passionately meeting each new goal that I create for myself is exciting!

As I wrote this book, it freed me from my pain and the past more and more each chapter and rewrite. It lightened my spirit and made me excited to see what I would be brave and bold enough to share next. It stoked a fiery passion and intense enthusiasm to peel the onion of my life.

It allowed me to stop living in the past and allow myself the ability to recognize my growth. It helped me heal.

To anyone out there who is searching for healing generational trauma, anxiety, depression, or for increasing self-worth and self-love, read this book with an open and honest heart. Turn the pages enthusiastically as you note what resonates within you and what demons you have already slain within. Get excited about it! Stay energized! Stay fierce! Stay devoted to yourself!

CHECK IN #4

Work is never done. There is always something more you could or should do. I learned that I could share so many experiences that hopefully help others not make my mistakes. I learned to heal my inner child and let her rest. I learned that the woman that I am is incredible as I am. Not everyone will understand me or how I choose to move in this world and that's perfectly okay. I learned that I should not take on other people's problems as my own.

It's not my job to teach you how to see me; it's my job to teach you how to treat me. I learned that allowing other people to treat me how they see fit directly reflects my feelings about myself. I learned not to give power to my past in my present to dictate my future. Instead, I learned to let go of people and situations that do not serve my growth and health.

I learned the journey is more important than the final destination. I am learning to let go of my fears by being open and honest about them and not allowing others to manipulate them. I have learned to hold myself accountable for my negative actions. I learned to take life step-by-step. The unknowns of how this book is received is none of my business. I learned that my words matter and should be shared. I learned the power of positive transformation.

I learned that I smile more on the inside than on the outside. I learned that my friends are my family. I learned that my comfort zone no longer serves me. I have learned that you can't take everybody with you but appreciate their impact on your life and growth. I learned to love myself unconditionally.

I am still learning not to backburner my needs, thoughts, and deeds. I am learning not to second guess my gifts. I am learning my identity is important to me and is constantly being redefined and refined as I show up more authentically each day.

I earned my blessings. I am learning balance instead of extremity, and I am learning how to set positive boundaries.

I am learning that I am the exception regarding how I express my truth, not the rule. I no longer give my power to others nor allow other people's expectations of me to dictate who I am and how I will behave. Instead, I am learning to balance the personal and professional aspects of telling my story. I am learning how motivational my quiet journey is for lots of people.

I am doing quite well by storytelling, affirming, and motivating myself and others.

I am.

CONCLUSION

I wrote this book to help start new and positive cycles in your life. You are not alone. I have, as well as many others, have been through many things that no one would believe or understand. We could all use a little positive reinforcement, as well as a place to share our burdens and our blessings. They are here and more are coming.

Let this book be your place of rest, your place to cry or write. Let its words encourage you to share your feelings with others and uplift one another.

We all need each other, and most importantly, we need self-love. I hope this book builds whatever tried to break you.

MANTRA

Here is my mantra from 2020, and I continue to use it. If it helps, use it, modify it, let it guide you to your place of peace.

I am a strong woman
Everything that has hit me in life, I've dealt with.
I've cried myself to sleep many nights
Picked me back up
And wiped away my own tears
I've grown from things meant to break me
I get stronger by the day
And I have spirit and the whole Universe to thank for that
This year I have 2020 vision
And I can see all my heart's desires
Clearly in front of me
Being manifested rapidly into my physical reality
This year I am too blessed to be stressed

www.ingramcontent.com/pod-product-compliance
Lightning Source LLC
Chambersburg PA
CBHW070912080526
44589CB00013B/1271